Cambridge Plain Texts

GOWER

CONFESSIO AMANTIS
SELECTIONS

CAMBRIDGE   UNIVERSITY   PRESS

LONDON : FETTER LANE, E.C.4

NEW YORK : THE MACMILLAN CO.

BOMBAY
CALCUTTA } MACMILLAN AND CO., LTD.
MADRAS

TORONTO : THE MACMILLAN CO. OF
            CANADA, LTD.

TOKYO : MARUZEN-KABUSHIKI-KAISHA

GOWER

CONFESSIO AMANTIS
SELECTIONS

CAMBRIDGE
AT THE UNIVERSITY PRESS
1927

PRINTED IN GREAT BRITAIN

INTRODUCTION

J. R. LOWELL, in his famous essay on Chaucer,
struck a blow at Gower's reputation from which
it has never fully recovered. Perhaps Chaucer's
phrase, "O, moral Gower," has not helped; al-
though, as W. P. Ker has well said, "There is more
wickedness in Gower than is commonly suspected."
Certainly Gower cannot be neglected by the student
of English literature, for he presents a most
interesting comparison with Chaucer, and we may
find in his work much that we find in that of
Chaucer: technical accomplishment, ability to
conduct his narrative with economy and skill,
and a directness of style, combined with occa-
sional flashes of forceful and picturesque imagery.
But he lacks those qualities which make Chaucer's
work so distinctive: he has little humour, no
considerable sense of drama, and, above all, his
work fails to give us that perpetual impression we
receive in reading almost any page of Chaucer,
of being in the presence of a loveable and wise
observer. At best, "Gower is what Chaucer might
have been without genius and without his Italian
reading, but with his critical tact, and much of
his skill in verse and diction."

The text printed here is taken with few changes
from the three-volume edition of R. Pauli of 1857.
Since then, the Gower canon has been exhaustively

studied by G. C. Macaulay, and a definitive edition of the whole of Gower's works, including the long-lost French poem, *Speculum Meditantis*, was published by him in four volumes in 1899–1902. The text used by Mr Macaulay for the *Confessio Amantis* is in many respects superior to that used by earlier editors, but the differences are not serious enough to prevent the lover of literature from finding ample enjoyment in a selection founded on less perfect editions.

H. S. B.

August, 1927

SELECTIONS

FROM THE
CONFESSIO AMANTIS

PART ONE

I. THE LOVER & THE CONFESSOR

[BOOK I, lines 93–288]

Upon the point that is befalle
Of love, in which that I am falle,
I thenke telle my matere.
Nowe herken, who that woll it here,
Of my fortune how that it ferde.
This enderday, as I forth ferde
To walke, as I you telle may,
And that was in the moneth of May,
Whan every brid hath chose his make
And thenketh his merthes for to make
Of love, that he hath acheved.
But so was I no thing releved,
For I was further fro my love
Than erthe is fro the hevene above,
And for to speke of any spede
So wiste I me none other rede,
But as it were a man forfare
Unto the wood I gan to fare,
Nought for to singe with the briddes,
For whan I was the wood amiddes
I fonde a swote grene pleine,
And there I gan my wo compleine
Wisshinge and wepinge all min one,

For other mirthes made I none.
So hard me was that ilke throwe,
That ofte sithes overthrowe
To grounde I was withoute brethe,
And ever I wisshed after dethe,
Whan I out of my peine awoke,
And caste up many a pitous loke
Unto the heven and saide thus:
'O thou Cupide, O thou Venus,
Thou god of love and thou goddesse,
Where is pite? where is mekenesse?
Now doth me pleinly live or die,
For certes suche a maladie
As I now have, and longe have had,
It mighte make a wise man mad,
If that it shulde longe endure.
O Venus, quene of loves cure,
Thou life, thou lust, thou mannes hele,
Beholde my cause and my quarele,
And yef me some part of thy grace,
So that I may finde in this place,
If thou be gracious or none!'
And with that worde I seigh anone
The Kinge of Love and Quene bothe.
But he, that king, with eyen wrothe
His chere aweiward fro me caste
And forthe he passed atte laste.
But natheles er he forth wente
A firy dart me thought he hente
And threwe it through min herte rote.
In him fonde I none other bote,

For lenger list him nought to dwelle.
But she, whiche is the source and welle
Of wele or wo, that shal betide
To hem that loven, at that tide
Abode, but for to tellen here
She cast on me no goodly chere,
Thus netheles to me she saide:
'What art thou, sone?' And I abraide
Right as a man doth out of slepe,
And therof toke she right good kepe
And bad me nothing be adradde,
But for al that I was nought gladde,
For I ne sawe no cause why.
And eft she asketh, what was I?

I saide: 'A caitif that lyth here.
What wolde ye, my lady dere?
Shall I be hole or elles die?'

She saide: 'Telle thy maladie.
What is thy sore of which thou pleinest?
Ne hide it nought, for if thou feignest
I can do thee no medicine.'

'Madame, I am a man of thine,
That in thy Court have longe served,
And axe that I have deserved,
Some wele after my longe wo.'

And she began to loure tho,
And saide: 'There be many of you
Faitours, and so may be that thou
Art right suche one, and by faintise
Saist that thou hast me do service.'

And natheles she wiste wele
My word stood on an other whele
Withouten any faiterie.
But algate of my maladie
She bad me tell and say her trouthe.

'Madame, if ye wolde have routhe,'
Quod I, 'than wolde I telle you.'

'Say forth,' quod she, 'and telle me how,
Shewe me thy sikenesse every dele.'

'Madame, that can I do wele,
Be so my life therto wol laste.'

With that her loke on me she caste
And saide: 'In aunter if thou live,
My wille is first, that thou be shrive;
And natheles how that it is
I wot my selfe, but for all this
Unto my Prest which cometh anone
I wol thou telle it one and one,
Both al thy thought and al thy werke.
O Genius, min owne clerke,
Come forth, and here this mannes shrifte,'
Quod Venus tho. And I uplifte
Min hede with that, and gan beholde
The selfe Prest, whiche as she wolde
Was redy there and fet him doune
To here my Confession.

This worthy prest, this holy man
To me spekend thus began
And saide: 'Benedicite
My sone, of the felicite

Of Love and eke of all the wo
Thou shalt be shrive of bothe two:
What thou er this for loves sake
Hast felt, let nothing be forsake;
Tel pleinly as it is befalle.'

And with that worde I gan down falle
On knees, and with devocion,
And with full great contricion,
I saide thanne! 'Dominus,
Min holy fader Genius,
So as thou haste experience
Of Love, for whose reverence
Thou shalt me shriven at this time,
I pray thee let me nought mistime
My shrifte, for I am destourbed
In all min herte and so contourbed,
That I ne may my wittes gete,
So shal I moche thing foryete.
But if thou wolt my shrifte oppose
Fro point to pointe, than I suppose
There shall nothing be left behinde.
But now my wittes be so blinde,
That I ne can my selfe teche.'

Tho he beganne anon to preche,
And with his wordes debonaire
He saide to me softe and faire:
My sone, I am assigned here
Thy shrifte to oppose and here
By Venus the goddesse above,
Whose prest I am touchend of love.

But natheles for certain skill
I mote algate and nedes will
Nought only make my spekinges
Of Love, but of other thinges
That touchen to the cause of Vice.
For that belongeth to thoffice
Of Prest, whose ordre that I bere:
So that I wol nothing forbere
That I the Vices one and one
Ne shall thee shewen everichone,
Wherof thou might take evidence
To reule with thy conscience.
But of conclusion finall
Conclude I wolde in speciall
For Love, whose servaunt I am
And why the cause is that I cam.
So thenke I to do bothe two,
First that min ordre longeth to
The Vices for to telle a rewe:
But nexte, above all other, shewe
Of Love I wol the propretes,
How that they stonde by degres
After the disposicion
Of Venus, whose condicion
I must folwe as I am holde,
For I with Love am al witholde,
So that the lasse I am to wite,
Though I ne conne but a lite
Of other thinges that bene wise,
I am nought taught in suche a wise.
For it is nought my comun use

To speke of vices and vertuse,
But all of Love and of his lore,
For Venus bokes of no more
Me techen, nouther text ne glose.
But for als moche as I suppose
It sit a Prest to be wel thewed
And shame it is if he be lewed,
Of my presthode after the forme
I wol thy shrifte so enforme,
That at the laste thou shalt here
The Vices, and to thy matere
Of Love I shal hem so remene
That thou shalt knowe what they mene.
For what a man shall axe or seine
Touchend of shrifte, it mot be pleine.
It nedeth nought to make it queinte,
For Trouth his wordes wol nought peinte.
That I wol axe of the forthy,
My sone, it shal be so pleinly
That thou shalt knowe and understonde
The pointes of shrifte how that they stonde.

II. THE TALE OF ALBINUS
AND ROSEMUND

[BOOK I, lines 2459–2661]

Of hem that we Lombardes now calle
Albinus was the firste of alle
Which bare crowne of Lombardie,
And was of great chivalerie
In werre ayeinst divers kinges.

So felle amonges other thinges,
That he that time a werre had
With Gurmund, which the Geptes lad,
And was a mightie kinge also.
But natheles it fell him so
Albinus slough him in the felde,
Ther halpe him nouther spere ne shelde,
That he ne smote his heved of thanne,
Wherof he toke away the panne,
Of whiche he saide he wolde make
A cuppe for Gurmundes sake
To kepe and drawe into memoire
Of his bataile the victoire.
And thus when he the felde had wonne,
The londe anon was overronne
And sesed in his owne honde;
Where he Gurmundes doughter fonde,
Which maide Rosemunde hight,
And was in every mannes sight
A fair, a fressh, a lusty one.
His herte fell to her anone,
And suche a love on her he cast,
That he her wedded atte last.
And after that long time in reste
With her he dwelleth, and to the beste
They love eche other wonder wele.
But she that kepeth the blinde whele,
Venus, when they be most above
In all the hottest of her love,
Her whele she torneth, and they felle
In the maner, as I shall telle.

This king, which stood in all his welth
Of pees, of worship and of helth,
And felt him on no side greved
As he that hath his worlde acheved,
Tho thought he wolde a feste make
And that was for his wives sake,
That she the lordes atte feste,
That were obeisaunt to his heste,
May knowe. And so forth there upon
He lette ordeigne and send anon
By letters and by messengers
And warned all his officers,
That every thing be well arraied,
The greate stedes were assaied
For justinge and for tornement,
And many a perled garnement
Embrouded as ayein the day.
The lordes in her beste array
Be comen at the time set;
One justeth well, an other bet,
And other while they torney;
And thus they casten care awey
And token lustes upon honde.
And after, thou shalt understonde,
To mete into the kinges halle
They comen, as they be bidden alle.
And whan they were set and served
Than after, as it was deserved
To hem that worthy knightes were,
So as they setten here and there,
The prise was yove and spoken out

Among the heralds all about.
And thus benethe and eke above
All was of armes and of love,
Wherof abouten atte bordes
Men hadde many sondry wordes,
That of the mirthe which they made
The kinge him self began to glade
Within his hert and toke a pride
And sigh the cuppe stonde aside,
Which made was of Gurmundes hed,
As ye have herd, when he was ded,
And was with golde and riche stones
Beset and bounde for the nones,
And stode upon a fote on highte
Of burned golde, and with great slighte
Of werkmenship it was begrave
Of such worke as it shulde have
And was policed eke so clene
That no signe of the scull was sene
But as it were a gripes eye.
The king bad bere his cuppe awey
Which stood before him on the borde
And fette thilke. Upon his worde
The sculle is fette and wine therinne,
Wherof he bad his wife beginne:
'Drink with thy fader, dame,' he said.
And she to his bidding obeid
And toke the sculle, and what her list
She drank, as she which nothing wist
What cup it was. And than all out
The kinge in audience about

Hath tolde it was her faders sculle,
So that the lordes knowe shulle
Of his bataile a soth witnesse,
And made avaunt through what prowesse
He hath his wives love wonne,
Whiche of the sculle hath so begonne.
Tho was there mochel Pride alofte,
They spoken all, and she was softe,
Thenkend on thilke unkinde Pride,
Of that her lord, so nigh her side,
Avaunteth him that he hath slaine
And piked out her faders braine,
And of the sculle had made a cuppe.
She suffreth all till they were uppe,
And tho she hath sekenesse feigned,
And goth to chambre and hath compleigned
Unto a maide which she triste,
So that none other wight it wiste.
This maide Glodeside is hote,
To whom this lady hath behote,
Of ladiship all that she can,
To vengen her upon this man,
Which did her drink in suche a plite
Among hem alle for despite
Of her and of her fader bothe;
Wherof her thoughtes ben so wrothe,
She saith, that she shall nought be glad,
Till that she se him so bestad
That he no more make avaunt.
And thus they felle in covenaunt,
That they accorden atte laste

With suche wiles as they caste,
That they wol get of here accorde
Some orped knight to sle this lorde.
And with this sleighte they beginne,
How they Helmege mighten winne,
Which was the kinges boteler,
A proude and lusty bachiler,
And Glodeside he loveth hote.
And she to make him more assote
Her love graunteth, and by nighte
They shape how they to-gider mighte
A bedde mete. And done it was
This same night. And in this cas
The quene her self the night seconde
Went in her stede, and there she fonde
A chambre derke without light,
And goth to bedde to this knight.
And he, to kepe his observaunce,
To love doth his obeisaunce,
And weneth it be Glodeside.
And she than after lay a side
And axeth him what he hath do,
And who she was she tolde him tho,
And said: 'Helmege, I am thy quene,
Now shall thy love well be sene
Of that thou hast thy wille wrought;
Or it shall sore ben abought,
Or thou shalt worche, as I thee saie.
And if thou wolt by suche a waie
Do my plesaunce and holde it stille,
For ever I shall ben at thy wille,

Bothe I and all min heritage.'
  Anone the wilde loves rage,
In which no man him can governe,
Hath made him that he can nought werne,
But felle all hole to her assent,
And thus the whele is all miswent,
The which Fortune hath upon honde.
For how that ever it after stonde,
They shope among hem such a wile
The king was ded within a while.
So slily came it nought aboute,
That they ne ben discovered out,
So that it thought hem for the beste
To fle, for there was no reste.
And thus the tresor of the kinge
They trusse, and mochel other thinge,
And with a certaine felaship
They fled and went awey by ship,
And helde her right cours from thenne,
Till that they comen to Ravenne,
Where they the dukes helpe sought.
And he, so as they him besought,
A place graunteth for to dwelle.
But after, whan he herde telle
Of the maner how they have do,
The duke let shape for hem so,
That of a poison which they drunke
They hadden that they have beswunke.
And all this made avaunt of Pride.
Good is therfore a man to hide
His owne prise, for if he speke,

He may lightly his thanke breke.
In armes lith none avauntance
To him, which thenketh his name avaunce
And be renomed of his dede.
And also who that thenketh to spede
Of Love he may nought him avaunte.
For what man thilke Vice haunte,
His purpose shall full ofte faile.
In armes he that woll travaile
Or elles Loves grace atteigne,
His lose tunge he mot restreigne,
Whiche bereth of his honour the keie.

III. THE TRAVELLERS AND THE ANGEL

[BOOK II, lines 291–372]

Of Jupiter thus I finde iwrite,
How whilom that he wolde wite
Upon the pleintes whiche he herde
Among the men, how that it ferde,
As of her wrong condicion
To do justificacion.
And for that cause down he sent
An aungel, which aboute went,
That he the sothe knowe may.
So it befell upon a day
This aungel, which him shuld enforme,
Was clothed in a mannes forme
And overtoke, I understonde,
Two men that wenten over londe,

Through which he thoughte to aspie
His cause, and goth in compaignie.
This aungel with his wordes wise
Opposeth hem in sondry wise,
Now loude wordes and now softe,
That made hem to desputen ofte.
And eche of hem his reson hadde.
And thus with tales he hem ladde
With good examinacion,
Till he knew the condicion
What men they were bothe two;
And sigh wel atte laste tho,
That one of hem was coveitous,
And his felaw was envious.
And thus, whan he hath knouleching,
Anone he feigned departing,
And said he mote algate wende.
But herken now what fell at ende,
For than he made hem understonde,
That he was there of Goddes sonde,
And said hem for the kindeship,
That they have done him felaship,
He wolde do some grace ayein,
And bad that one of hem shuld sain
What thinge him is levest to crave,
And he it shall of yifte have.
And over that eke forth with all
He saith that other have shall
The double of that his felawe axeth:
And thus to hem his grace he taxeth.
The coveitous was wonder glad,

And to that other man he bad
And saith, that he first axe sholde;
For he supposeth that he wolde
Make his axing of worldes good;
For than he knewe well howe it stood,
That he him self by double weight
Shall efte take, and thus by sleight,
By cause that he wolde winne,
He badde his felaw first beginne.
This envious, though it be late
Whan that he sigh he mote algate
Make his axinge first, he thought
If he worship or profit sought,
It shall be doubled to his fere:
That wold he chese in no manere.
But than he sheweth what he was
Towarde Envie, and in this cas
Unto this aungel thus he saide
And for his yifte this he praide,
To make him blinde on his one eye,
So that his felaw no thing sigh.
This word was nought so sone spoke,
That his one eye anon was loke,
And his felaw forth with also
Was blinde on both his eyen two.
Tho was that other gladde inough,
That one wept, and that other lough,
He set his one eye at no cost
Wherof that other two hath lost
Of thilke ensample, which fell tho,
Men tellen now full ofte so.

The worlde empeireth comunly
And yet wot none the cause why;
For it accordeth nought to kinde
Min owne harme to seche and finde,
Of that I shall my brother greve
I mighte never wel acheve.

IV. THE TALE OF CEIX & ALCEONE

[BOOK IV, lines 2927-3123]

This finde I writen in poesy.
Ceix the king of Troceny
Hadde Alceone to his wife,
Which as her owne hertes life
Him loveth. And he had also
A brother, which was cleped tho
Dedalion, and he par cas
Fro kinde of man forshape was
Into a goshauke for likenesse;
Wherof this king great hevinesse
Hath take and thought in his corage
To gone upon a pelrinage
Into a straunge region,
Where he hath his devocion
To done his sacrifice and prey,
If that he might in any wey
Toward the goddes finde grace
His brothers hele to purchace,
So that he mighte be reformed
Of that he hadde be transformed.
To this purpose and to this ende

This king is redy for to wende
As he which wolde go by ship.
And for to done him felaship
His wife unto the see him brought
With all her herte, and him besought
That he the time her wolde sein
Whan that he thoughte come ayein.
'Within,' he saith, 'two monthes day.'
And thus in alle haste he may
He toke his leve and forth he saileth
Wepend, and she her self bewaileth
And torneth home there she cam fro.
But whan the monthes were ago,
The which he set of his coming,
And that she herde no tiding,
There was no care for to seche:
Wherof the goddes to beseche
Tho she began in many a wise,
And to Juno her sacrifice
Above all other most she dede,
And for her lord she hath so bede
To wite and knowe how that he ferd,
That Juno the goddesse her herde
Anone, and upon this matere
She badde Yris her messagere
To Slepes hous that she shal wende,
And bid him that he make an ende
By sweven, and shewe all the cas
Unto this lady how it was.

     This Yris, fro the highe stage
Whiche undertake hath the message,

Her reiny cope did upon,
The which was wonderly begone
With colours of diverse hewe
An hunderd mo than men it knewe,
The heven liche unto a bowe
She bende, and she cam downe lowe,
The God of Slepe where that she fond,
And that was in a straunge lond
Which marcheth upon Chimery.
For there, as saith the poesy,
The God of Slepe hath made his hous,
Whiche of entaile is merveilous.

Under an hill there is a cave,
Which of the sonne may nought have,
So that no man may knowe aright
The point betwene the day and night.
There is no fire, there is no sparke,
There is no dore which may charke,
Wherof an eye shulde unshet,
So that inward there is no let.
And for to speke of that withoute,
There stant no great tre nigh aboute,
Wheron there mighte crowe or pie
Alighte for to clepe or crie.
There is no cock to crowe day,
Ne beste none which noise may
The hille, but all aboute round
There is growend upon the ground
Poppy, which bereth the sede of slepe,
With other herbes suche an hepe.
A stille water for the nones

Rennend upon the smalle stones,
Which hight of Lethes the river,
Under that hille in such maner
There is, which yiveth great appetite
To slepe. And thus ful of delite
Slepe hath his hous, and of his couche
Within his chambre if I shall touche,
Of hebenus that slepy tre
The bordes all aboute be,
And for he shulde slepe softe
Upon a fether bed alofte
He lith with many a pilwe of doun:
The chambre is strowed up and doun
With swevenes many a thousand fold.
Thus came Yris into this holde
And to the bed, whiche is all black,
She goth, and ther with Slepe she spake,
And in this wise as she was bede
The message of Juno she dede.
Full ofte her wordes she reherceth,
Er she his slepy eres perceth
With mochel wo. But atte laste
His slombrend eyen he upcaste
And said her that it shal be do.
Wherof amonge a thousand tho
Within his hous that slepy were
In speciall he chese out there
Thre, whiche shulden do this dede.
The first of hem, so as I rede,
Was Morpheus, the whose nature
Is for to take the figure

Of that persone that him liketh,
Wherof that he ful ofte entriketh
The life which slepe shal by night.
And Ithecus that other hight,
Which hath the vois of every soun,
The chere and the condicioun
Of every life, what so it is.
The thridde suend after this
Is Panthasas, which may transforme
Of every thing the righte forme
And chaunge it in another kinde.
Upon hem thre, so as I finde,
Of swevens stant all thapparence,
Which other while is evidence
And other while but a jape.
But natheles it is so shape,
That Morpheus by night alone
Appereth unto Alceone
In likenesse of her husebonde
Al naked dede upon the stronde,
And how he dreint in speciall
These other two it shewen all.
The tempest of the blacke cloude
The wode see, the windes loude,
All this she met, and sigh him deien,
Wherof that she began to crien
Slepend abedde there she lay.
And with that noise of her affray
Her women sterten up aboute,
Whiche of her lady were in doubte
And axen her how that she ferde.

And she, right as she sigh and herde,
Her sweven hath tolde hem every dele.
And they it halsen alle wele
And sain, it is a token of good;
But til she wist how that it stood,
She hath no comfort in her herte.
Upon the morwe and up she sterte
And to the see where as she mete
The body lay, withoute lete
She drough, and whanne she cam nigh,
Starke dede, his armes sprad, she sigh
Her lord fletend upon the wawe.
Wherof her wittes be withdrawe,
And she which toke of deth no kepe,
Anone forth lepte into the depe
And wold have caught him in her arme.
This infortune of double harme
The goddes from the heven above
Beheld, and for the trouthe of love,
Whiche in this worthy lady stood,
They have upon the salte flood
Her dreinte lorde and her also
Fro deth to life torned so,
That they ben shapen into briddes
Swimmend upon the wawe amiddes.
And whan she sigh her lord livend
In likenesse of a bird swimmend,
And she was of the same sort,
So as she mighte do disport
Upon the joie which she hadde,
Her winges both abrode she spradde

And him, so as she may suffise,
Beclipt and kist in suche a wise
As she was whilome wont to do.
Her winges for her armes two
She toke, and for her lippes softe
Her harde bille, and so ful ofte
She fondeth in her briddes forme,
If that she might her self conforme
To do the plesaunce of a wife,
As she did in that other life.
For though she hadde her power lore
Her will stood as it was to-fore,
And serveth him so as she may.
Wherof into this ilke day
To-gider upon the see they wone,
Where many a doughter and a sone
They bringen forth of briddes kinde.
And for men shulden take in minde
This Alceon the trewe quene,
Her briddes yet, as it is sene,
Of Alceon the name bere.

V. THE TALE OF JASON & MEDEA

[BOOK V, lines 3247 4222]

In Grece whilom was a king,
Of whom the fame and knouleching
Beleveth yet, and Peleus
He highte, but it fell him thus,
That his fortune her whele so lad,
That he no childe his owne had

To regnen after his decess.
He had a brother natheles,
Whose righte name was Eson,
And he the worthy knight Jason
Begat, the which in every londe
All other passed of his honde
In armes, so that he the best
Was named and the worthiest,
He soughte worship over all.
Now herken, and I telle shall
An adventure that he sought,
Which afterward full dere he bought.

    There was an ile, which Colchos
Was cleped, and therof aros
Great speche in every londe aboute,
That such merveile was none oute
In all the wide world no where,
As tho was in that ile there.
There was a shepe, as it was tolde,
The which his flees bare all of golde,
And so the goddes had it sette
That it ne might away be fette
By power of no worldes wight.
And yet full many a worthy knight
It had assaied, as they dorste,
And ever it fell hem to the worste.
But he that wolde it nought forsake
But of his knighthode undertake
To do what thing therto belongeth,
This worthy Jason, sore alongeth
To se the straunge regions

And knowe the conditions
Of other marches where he went.
And for that cause his hole entent
He sette Colchos for to seche,
And therupon he made a speche
To Peleus his eme the king.
And he wel paid was of that thing,
And shope anone for his passage,
And such as were of his lignage,
With other knightes whiche he chees,
With him he toke, and Hercules
Which full was of chivalerie
With Jason went in compaignie;
And that was in the month of May
Whan colde stormes were away.
The wind was good, the ship was yare,
They toke her leve and forth they fare
Toward Colchos. But on the way
What hem befelle is long to say,
How Lamedon the king of Troy,
Which oughte well have made hem joy,
Whan they to rest a while him preide,
Out of his lond he them congeide.
And so fell the dissention,
Whiche after was destruction
Of that citee, as men may here.
But that is nought to my matere,
But thus the worthy folk Gregois
Fro that king which was nought curtois
And fro his londe with sail updrawe
They went hem forth, and many a sawe

They made and many a great manace;
Till atte last into that place
Which as they soughte they arrive,
And striken sail, and forth as blive
They sent unto the king and tolden
Who weren there and what they wolden.
   Oetes, which was thanne king,
Whan that he herde this tiding
Of Jason, which was comen there,
And of these other, what they were,
He thoughte done him great worship.
For they anone come out of ship
And straught unto the king they wente
And by the honde Jason he hente,
And that was at the paleis gate,
So fer the king came on his gate
Toward Jason to done him chere.
And he, whom lacketh no manere,
Whan he the king sigh in presence,
Yaf him ayein such reverence
As to the kinges state belongeth.
And thus the king him underfongeth
And Jason in his arme he caught
And forth into the hall he straught,
And there they sit and speke of thinges
And Jason tolde him tho tidinges
Why he was come, and faire him preide
To haste his time, and the king seide:
   'Jason, thou art a worthy knight,
But it lieth in no mannes might
To done that thou art come fore.

There hath bene many a knight forlore
Of that they wolden it assaie.'
But Jason wolde him nought esmaie
And saide: 'Of every worldes cure
Fortune stant in aventure,
Paraunter well, paraunter wo.
But how as ever that it go,
It shall be with min honde assaied.'
The king tho helde him nought wel paied,
For he the Grekes sore dredde,
In aunter, if Jason ne spedde,
He mighte therof bere a blame;
For tho was all the worldes fame
In Grece, as for to speke of armes.
Forthy he drad him of his harmes
And gan to preche him and to prey.
But Jason wolde nought obey,
But said, he wolde his purpos holde
For ought that any man him tolde.
The king whan he these wordes herde
And sigh how that this knight answerde
Yet for he wolde make him glad,
After Medea gone he bad,
Which was his doughter, and she cam.
And Jason, which good hede nam,
Whan he her sigh ayein her goth.
And she, which was him nothing loth,
Welcomed him into that londe
And softe toke him by the honde
And down they setten bothe same.
She had herd spoken of his name

And of his grete worthinesse;
Forthy she gan her eye impresse
Upon his face and his stature,
And thought, how never creature
Was so welfarend as was he.
And Jason right in such degre
Ne mighte nought witholde his loke,
But so good hede on her he toke,
That him ne thought under the heven
Of beaute sigh he never her even,
With all that felle to womanhede.
Thus eche of other token hede
Though there no word was of recorde,
Her hertes both of one accorde
Ben sette to love, but as tho
There mighten ben no wordes mo.
The king made him great joy and fest,
To all his men he yaf an hest,
So as they wolde his thank deserve,
That they shulde alle Jason serve,
While that he wolde there dwelle.
And thus the day, shortly to telle,
With many merthes they dispent,
Till night was come, and tho they went;
Echone of other toke his leve,
Whan they no lenger mighten leve.
I not how Jason that night slepe,
But well I wot, that of the shepe
For which he cam into that ile
He thoughte but a litel while;
All was Medea that he thought,

So that in many wise he sought
His wit, wakend er it was day,
Some time ye, some time nay,
Some time thus, some time so,
As he was stered to and fro
Of love and eke of his conquest,
As he was holde of his behest.
And thus he rose up by the morwe
And toke him self seint John to borwe,
And saide, he wolde first beginne
At love, and after for to winne
The flees of gold for which he come,
And thus to him good herte he nome.
    Medea right the same wise
Till day cam, that she must arise,
Lay and bethought her all the night,
How she that noble worthy knight
By any waie mighte wedde.
And wel she wist, if he ne spedde
Of thing which he had undertake,
She might her self no purpose take.
For if he deiede of his bataile,
She muste than algate faile
To geten him, whan he were dede.
Thus she began to sette rede
And torne about her wittes all
To loke how that it mighte fall,
That she with him had a leisir
To speke and telle of her desir.
And so it fell the same day
That Jason with that swete may

To-gider set and hadden space
To speke, and he besought her grace.
And she his tale goodly herde,
And afterward she him answerde
And saide: 'Jason, as thou wilt
Thou might be sauf, thou might be spilt,
For witte well, that never man,
But if he couthe that I can,
Ne mighte that fortune acheve,
For which thou comest. But as I leve,
If thou wolt holde covenaunt
To love, of all the remenaunt
I shall thy life and honour save,
That thou the flees of gold shalt have.'
He said: 'Al at your owne wille,
Madame, I shall truly fulfille
Your heste, while my life may last.'
Thus longe he praid, and atte last
She graunteth, and behight him this,
That whan night cometh and it time is
She wolde him sende certainly
Such one that shulde him prively
Alone into her chambre bringe.
He thonketh her of that tidinge,
For of that grace is him begonne
Him thenketh al other thinges wonne.

The day made ende and lost his light
And comen was the derke night,
Whiche all the daies eye blent.
Jason toke leve and forth he went,
And whan he cam out of the prees,

He toke to counseil Hercules
And tolde him how it was betid,
And praide it shulde well ben hid,
And that he wolde loke about
The whiles that he shall be out.
Thus as he stood and hede name,
A maiden fro Medea came,
And to her chambre Jason ledde,
Where that he found redy to bedde
The fairest and the wisest eke.
And she with simple chere and meke,
Whan she him sigh, wax all ashamed.
Tho was her tale newe entamed
For sikernesse of mariage,
She fette forth a riche ymage,
Was the figure of Jupiter,
And Jason swore and saide there,
That also wis god shuld him helpe,
That if Medea did him helpe,
That he his purpose mighte winne,
They shulde never part atwinne,
But ever while him lasteth life,
He wolde holde her for his wife.

*   *   *   *   *

They hadden bothe what they wolde.
And than at leiser she him tolde,
And gan fro point to point enforme
Of this bataile and all the forme,
Whiche as he shulde finde there,
Whan he to thile come were.

She saide, at entre of the pas
How Mars, which God of Armes was,
Hath set two oxen sterne and stoute,
That casten fire and flame aboute
Both ate mouth and at the nase,
So that they setten all on blase
What thing that passeth hem betwene.
And furthermore upon the grene
There goth, the flees of gold to kepe,
A serpent which may never slepe.
Thus who that ever it shulde winne,
The fire to stoppe he mot beginne
Which that the fierce bestes caste,
And daunt he mot hem atte laste,
So that he may hem yoke and drive;
And there upon he mot as blive
The serpent with such strength assaile,
That he may sleen him by bataile,
Of which he mot the teeth outdrawe,
As it belongeth to that lawe.
And than he must the oxen yoke
Til they have with a plough to-broke
A furgh of lond, in which arow
The teeth of thadder he must sow.
And therof shull arise knightes
Well armed at alle rightes;
Of hem in nought to taken hede,
For eche of hem in hastihede
Shall other slee with dethes wounde.
And thus whan they ben laid to grounde
Than mot he to the goddes pray

And go so forth and take his pray.
But if he faile in any wise
Of that ye here me devise,
There may be set non other wey,
That he ne must algates deie.
'Now have I told the peril all
I woll you tellen forth withall,'
Quod Medea to Jason tho,
'That ye shull knowen er ye go
Ayein the venim and the yr,
What shall be the recoverir.
But, sire, for it is nigh day,
Ariseth up, so that I may
Deliver you what thing I have
That may your life and honour save.'

*   *   *   *   *

Tho toke she forth a riche tie
Made all of gold and of perrie,
Out of the which she nam a ring,
The stone was worth all other thing.
She saide, while he wold it were,
There mighte no peril him dere;
In water may it nought be dreint,
Where as it cometh the fire is queint,
It daunteth eke the cruel beste,
There may none quad that man areste,
Where so he be on see or londe,
That hath this ring upon his honde.
And over that she gan to sein,
That if a man will ben unsein,

Within his hond hold close the stone
And he may invisible gone.
The ring to Jason she betaught
And so forth after she him taught
What sacrifice he shulde make.
And gan out of her cofre take
Him thought an hevenly figure,
Which all by charme and by conjure
Was wrought, and eke it was through writ
With names, which he shulde wite,
As she him taughte tho to rede;
And bad him, as he wolde spede,
Withoute rest of any while,
Whan he were londed in that ile,
He shulde make his sacrifice
And rede his carect in the wise
As she him taught, on knees down bent
Thre sithes toward orient.
For so shuld he the goddes plese
And win him selven mochel ese.
And whan he had it thries radde
To open a buist she him badde,
That she there toke him in present,
And was full of such oignement
That there was fire ne venim non
That shulde fastne him upon,
Whan that he were anoint withall.
Forthy she taught him how he shall
Anoint his armes all aboute,
And for he shulde nothing doubte
She toke him than a maner glue,

The which was of so great vertue
That where a man it shulde cast
It shulde binde anon so fast
That no man might it done away.
And that she bad by alle way
He shulde into the mouthes throw
Of tho twein oxen that fire blow,
Therof to stoppen the malice
The glue shall serve of that office.
And over that, her oignement
Her ring and her enchauntement
Ayein the serpent shulde him were,
Till he him slee with swerd or spere.
And than he may saufly inough
His oxen yoke into the plough
And the teeth sowe in such a wise
Till he the knightes se arise,
And eche of other down be laide
In suche a maner as I have saide.
    Lo, thus Medea for Jason
Ordeineth, and praieth therupon
That he nothing foryete sholde,
And eke she praieth him that he wolde,
Whan he hath all his armes done,
To grounde knele and thonke anone
The goddes, and do forth by ese
The flees of golde he shulde sese.
And whan he had it sesed so,
That than he were sone ago
Withouten any tarieng.
Whan this was said, into weping

She fel, as she that was throughnome
With love, and so fer overcome,
That all her worlde on him she sette.
But whan she sigh there was no lette,
That he mot nedes part her fro,
She toke him in her armes two
An hunderd times and gan him kisse,
And said: 'O, all my worldes blisse,
My trust, my lust, my life, min hele,
To ben thin helpe in this quarele
I pray unto the goddes alle!'
And with that word she gan down falle
Of swoune, and he her uppe nam,
And forth with that the maiden cam,
And they to bed anone her brought,
And thanne Jason her besought
And to her saide in this manere:
'My worthy lusty lady dere,
Comforteth you, for by my trouth
It shall nought fallen in my slouth
That I ne woll throughout fulfille
Your hestes at your owne wille.
And yet I hope to you bringe
Within a while such tidinge,
The which shall make us bothe game.'

      But for he wolde kepe her name,
Whan that he wist it was nigh day,
He saide, 'Adewe my swete may.'
And forth with him he nam his gere
Which as she hadde take him there,
And straught unto his chambre went

And goth to bedde and slepe him hent,
And lay, that no man him awoke,
For Hercules hede of him toke,
Till it was underne high and more.
And than he gan to sighe sore
And sodeinlich he braide of slepe;
And they than token of him kepe,
His chamberleins, ben sone there
And maden redy all his gere,
And he arose and to the king
He went, and said how to that thing
For which he cam he wolde go.
The king therof was wonder wo,
And for he wolde him fain withdraw,
He told him many a dredefull sawe.
But Jason wolde it nought recorde
And ate laste they accorde.
Whan that he wolde nought abide,
A bote was redy ate tide,
In which this worthy knight of Grece,
Full armed up at every piece,
To his bataile which belongeth,
Toke ore in hond and sore him longeth
Till he the water passed were.
    Whan he cam to that ile there,
He set him on his knees down straught
And his carecte, as he was taught,
He rad and made his sacrifice,
And sith anoint him in that wise,
As Medea him hadde bede;
And than arose up fro that stede,

And with the glue the fire he queint;
And anone after he atteint
The grete serpent and him slough.
But erst he hadde sorwe inough,
For that serpent made him travaile
So hard and sore of his bataile,
That now he stood and nowe he fell,
For longe time it so befell,
That with his swerd and with his spere
He mighte nought that serpent dere,
He was so sherded all aboute
It held all egge tole withoute,
He was so rude and hard of skin
There might no thinge go therein.
Venim and fire to-gider he cast,
That he Jason so sore ablast
That if ne were his oignement,
His ring and his enchauntement,
Which Medea toke him before,
He hadde with that worm be lore.
But of vertu which therof cam
Jason the dragon overcam,
And he anone the teeth out drough
And set his oxen in his plough,
With which he brake a piece of lond
And sewe hem with his owne hond.
Tho might he great merveile se,
Of every toth in his degre
Sprong up a knight with spere and sheld,
Of which anone right in the feld
Echone slough other; and with that

Jason Medea not foryat,
On both his knees he gan down falle
And yaf thank to the goddes alle.
The flees he toke and goth to bote,
The sonne shineth bright and hote,
The flees of gold shone forth with all,
The water glistreth over all.
Medea wept and sigheth ofte
And stood upon a toure alofte;
Al prively within her selve,
There herd it nouther ten ne twelve,
She praid, and said: 'O, god him spede,
The knight which hath my maidenhede!'
And ay she loketh toward thile,
But whan she sigh within a while
The flees glistrend ayein the sonne,
She said: 'Ha lord, now all is wonne,
My knight the feld hath overcome;
Now wolde god, he were come.
Ha lord, I wold he were alonde!'
But I dare take this on honde,
If that she hadde winges two,
She wold have flowe unto him tho
Straught there he was unto the bote.
The day was clere, the sonne hote,
The Gregois weren in great doubt,
The while that her lord was out,
They wisten nought what shuld betide,
But waited ever upon the tide
To see what ende shulde falle.
There stoden eke the nobles alle

Forth with the comunes of the town,
And as they loken up and down,
They weren ware within a throwe
Where cam the bote, which they wel knowe,
And sigh how Jason brought his prey.
And tho they gonnen alle say
And criden alle with o steven:
'Ha, where was ever under the heven
So noble a knight as Jason is?'
And wel nigh alle saiden this,
That Jason was a faire knight,
For it was never of mannes might
The flees of gold so for to winne,
And thus to tellen they beginne.
With that the king cam forth anone
And sigh the flees, how that it shone.
And whan Jason cam to the londe,
The kinge him selve toke his honde
And kist him and great joy him made.
The Gregois weren wonder glade
And of that thing right merry hem thought
And forth with hem the flees they brought,
And eche on other gan to ligh.
But wel was him that mighte nigh
To se there of the proprete,
And thus they passen the citee
And gone unto the paleis straught.

    Medea, which foryat her nought,
Was redy there and said anon:
'Welcome, O worthy knight Jason!'
She wolde have kist him wonder fain,

But shame torned her ayain;
It was nought the manere as tho,
Forthy she dorste nought do so.
She toke her leve, and Jason went
Into his chambre, and she him sent
Her maiden to sene how he ferde.
The which whan that she sigh and herde,
How that he hadde faren out
And that it stood well all about,
She tolde her lady what she wist,
And she for joy her maiden kist.
The bathes weren than araied,
With herbes tempred and assaied,
And Jason was unarmed sone
And dide as it befell to done;
Into his bathe he went anone
And wisshe him clene as any bone;
He toke a soppe and out he cam
And on his best array he nam
And kempt his hede, whan he was clad,
And goth him forth all merry and glad
Right straught into the kinges halle.
The king cam with his knightes alle
And maden him glad welcoming.
And he hem tolde tho tiding
Of this and that, how it befell,
Whan that he wan the shepes fell.
Medea, whan she was asent,
Come sone to that parlement,
And whan she mighte Jason se,
Was none so glad of all as she.

There was no joie for to seche,
Of him made every man a speche,
Some man said one, some said other,
But though he were goddes brother
And mighte make fire and thonder,
There mighte be no more wonder
Than was of him in that citee.
Echone taught other 'This is he
Whiche hath in his power withinne
That all the world ne mighte winne:
Lo, here the best of alle good!'
Thus saiden they, that there stood
And eke that walked up and down
Both of the court and of the town.

The time of souper cam anon,
They wisshen and therto they gon;
Medea was with Jason set,
Tho was there many a deinte fet
And set to-fore hem on the bord,
But none so liking as the word
Which was there spoke among hem two,
So as they dorste speke tho.
But though they hadden litel space,
Yet they accorden in that place
How Jason shulde come at night,
Whan every torche and every light
Were out, and than of other thinges
They speke aloud for supposinges
Of hem that stoden there aboute:
For love is evermore in doubte,
If that it be wisly governed

Of hem that ben of love lerned.
Whan al was done, that dissh and cup
And cloth and bord and all was up,
They waken while hem list to wake,
And after that they leve take
And gon to bedde for to reste.
And whan him thoughte for the beste,
That every man was fast a slepe,
Jason, that wolde his time kepe,
Goth forth stalkend all prively
Unto the chambre and redely
There was a maide, which him kept.
Medea woke and no thing slept,

*   *   *   *   *

So that they hadden joy inow.
And tho they setten whan and how
That she with him awey shal stele,
With wordes such and other fele.
Whan all was treted to an ende,
Jason toke leve and gan forth wende
Unto his owne chambre in pees.
There wist it non but Hercules.

He slept and ros, whan it was time,
And whan it fel towardes prime,
He toke to him such as he triste
In secre, that none other wiste,
And told hem of his counseil there,
And saide that his wille were,
That they to ship had alle thing
So privelich in thevening,

That no man might her dede aspie
But tho that were of compaignie:
For he woll go withoute leve
And lenger woll he nought beleve,
But he ne wolde at thilke throwe
The king or quene shulde it knowe.
They said, 'All this shall well be do.'
And Jason truste well therto.

    Medea in the mene while,
Which thought her fader to beguile,
The tresor which her fader hadde
With her all prively she ladde,
And with Jason at time set
Away she stale and found no let,
And straught she goth her into ship
Of Grece with that felaship.
And they anone drough up the saile,
And all that night this was counseil.
But erly whan the sonne shone,
Men sigh how that they were gone
And come unto the kinge and tolde.
And he the sothe knowe wolde
And axeth, where his doughter was.
There was no word, but 'Out alas,
She was ago.' The moder wept,
The fader as a wodeman lept,
And gan the time for to warie,
And swore his othe he wold nought tarie,
That with caliphe and with galey
The same cours, the same wey,
Which Jason toke he wolde take,

If that he might him overtake.
To this they saiden alle ye.
Anone as they were ate see
And all as who saith at one worde,
They gone withinne shippes borde,
The sail goth up, and forth they straught,
But none esploit therof they caught,
And so they tornen home ayein,
For all that labour was in vein.
Jason to Grece with his pray
Goth through the see the righte way.
Whan he there come and men it tolde,
They maden joie yong and olde.

Eson, whan that he wist of this,
How that his sone comen is,
And hath acheved that he sought
And home with him Medea brought,
In all the wide world was none
So glad a man as he was one.
To-gider ben these lovers tho,
Till that they hadden sones two
Wherof they weren bothe glade,
And olde Eson great joie made
To seen thencrees of his lignage;
For he was of so great an age
That men awaiten every day
Whan that he shulde gone away.
Jason, which sigh his fader olde,
Upon Medea made him bolde
Of art magique which she couth,
And praieth her that his faders youth

She wolde make ayeinward newe.
And she that was toward him trewe
Behight him that she wolde it do,
Whan that she time sigh therto.
But what she did in that matere
It is a wonder thing to here,
But yet for the novellerie
I thenke tellen a great partie.

   Thus it befell upon a night,
Whan there was nought but sterre light,
She was vanisshed right as her list,
That no wight but her self it wist,
And that was ate midnight tide;
The world was still on every side,
With open hede and foot all bare
Her hair to-sprad she gan to fare,
Upon her clothes gert she was,
All specheles and on the gras
She glode forth as an adder doth.
None other wise she ne goth,
Till she came to the fresshe flood,
And there a while she withstood.
Thries she torned her aboute
And thries eke she gan down loute,
And in the flood she wete her hair,
And thries on the water there
She gaspeth with a drecchinge onde,
And tho she toke her speche on honde.
First she began to clepe and calle
Upwarde unto the sterres alle,
To winde, to air, to see, to londe

She preide and eke helde up her honde
To Echates and gan to crie,
Whiche is goddesse of sorcerie.
She saide, 'Helpeth at this nede,
And as ye maden me to spede
Whan Jason came the flees to seche,
So help me now, I you beseche!'
With that she loketh and was ware,
Down fro the sky there came a chare,
The which dragons aboute drowe.
And tho she gan her hede down bowe,
And up she stighe and faire and well
She drove forth by chare and wheel
Above in thaire among the skies;
The londe of Crete in tho parties
She sought, and faste gan her hie,
And therupon the hulles high
Of Othrin and Olimpe also,
And eke of other hulles mo,
She founde and gadreth herbes suote,
She pulleth up some by the rote,
And many with a knife she shereth,
And all into her char she bereth.
Thus whan she hath the hulles sought,
The floodes there foryate she nought
Eridian and Amphrisos,
Peneie and eke Spercheidos,
To hem she went and there she nome
Both of the water and of the fome,
The sonde and eke the smalle stones
Whiche as she chese out for the nones,

And of the Redde See a part,
That was behovelich to her art,
She toke, and after that about
She soughte sondry sedes out
In feldes and in many greves,
And eke a part she toke of leves.
But thing which might her most availe
She found in Crete and in Thessaile.
In daies and in nightes nine,
With great travaile and with great peine
She was purveyed of every piece
And torneth homward into Grece.
Before the gates of Eson
Her chare she let away to gone,
And toke out first that was therinne;
For tho she thoughte to beginne
Such thing as semeth impossible,
And made her selven invisible,
As she that was with thaire enclosed
And might of no man be desclosed.
She toke up turves of the londe
Withoute helpe of mannes honde,
And heled with the grene gras,
Of whiche an alter made there was
Unto Echates the goddesse
Of art magique and the maistresse.
And efte an other to Juvent,
As she which did her hole intent.
Tho toke she feldwode and verveine,
Of herbes ben nought better tweine,
Of which anone withoute let

These alters ben aboute set.
Two sondry pittes faste by
She made, and with that hastely
A wether which was black she slough,
And out therof the blood she drough
And did into the pittes two;
Warm milk she put also therto
With hony meind, and in such wise
She gan to make her sacrifice,
And cried and praide forth withall
To Pluto the god infernal,
And to the quene Proserpine.
And so she sought out all the line
Of hem that longen to that craft,
Behinde was no name last,
And praid hem all, as she well couth,
To graunt Eson his firste youth.
This olde Eson brought forth was tho,
Away she bad all other go
Upon peril that mighte falle;
And with that word they wenten alle
And left hem there two alone.
And tho she gan to gaspe and gone,
And made signes many one,
And said her wordes therupon,
And with spellinge and her charmes
She toke Eson in both her armes,
And made him for to slepe fast
And him upon her herbes cast.
The blacke wether tho she toke
And hew the flesshe as doth a coke;

On either alter part she laide,
And with the charmes that she saide
A fire down fro the sky alight
And made it for to brenne light.
And whan Medea sigh it brenne,
Anone she gan to sterte and renne
The firy alters all about.
There was no beste which goth out
More wilde than she semeth there.
Aboute her shulders heng her hair
As though she were oute of her minde
And torned to another kinde.
Tho lay there certain wode cleft,
Of which the pieces now and eft
She made hem in the pittes wete,
And put hem in the firy hete
And toke the bronde with all the blase,
And thries she began to rase
About Eson, there as he slept.
And eft with water, which she kept,
She made a cercle about him thries
And eft with fire of sulphre twies:
Full many another thing she dede,
Whiche is nought writen in the stede.
But tho she ran so up and doune
She made many a wonder soune,
Sometime lich unto the cock,
Sometime unto the laverock,
Sometime cacleth as an hen,
Sometime speketh as don men.
And right so as her jargon straungeth

In sondry wise her forme chaungeth,
She semeth faire and no woman:
For with the craftes that she can
She was, as who saith, a goddesse,
And what her liste, more or lesse,
She did, in bokes as we finde,
That passeth over mannes kinde.
But who that woll of wonders here,
What thing she wrought in this matere
To make an ende of that she gan,
Such merveil herde never man.

Apointed in the newe mone,
Whan it was time for to done,
She set a caldron on the fire,
In which was al the hole attire
Whereon the medicine stood,
Of juse, of water, and of blood,
And let it boile in suche a plite
Till that she sigh the spume white.
And tho she cast in rinde and rote
And sede and floure that was for bote,
With many an herbe and many a stone
Wherof she hath there many one.
And eke Cimpheius, the serpent,
To her hath all her scales lent,
Chelidre her yafe her adders skin,
And she to boilen cast hem in,
And parte eke of the horned oule,
The which men here on nightes houle,
And of a raven which was tolde
Of nine hundred winter olde

4-2

She toke the hede with all the bille.
And as the medicine it wille,
She toke her after the bowele
Of the seewolf, and for the hele
Of Eson, with a thousand mo
Of thinges that she hadde tho,
In that caldron to-gider as blive
She put, and toke than of olive
A drie braunche hem with to stere,
The which anon gan floure and bere
And waxe all fresshe and grene ayein.
Whan she this vertue hadde sene,
She let the leeste droppe of alle
Upon the bare floure down falle:
Anon there sprong up floure and gras
Where as the droppe fallen was,
And waxe anone all medow grene
So that it mighte well be sene.
Medea thanne knewe and wist
Her medicine is for to trist,
And goth to Eson there he lay
And toke a swerd was of assay,
With which a wounde upon his side
She made, that there out may slide
The blood withinne, which was olde
And sike and trouble and feble and colde.
And tho she toke unto his use
Of herbes all the beste juse,
And poured it into his wounde,
That made his veines full and sounde.
And tho she made his woundes close,

And toke his honde, and up he rose.
And tho she yaf him drinke a draught
Of which his youth ayein he caught,
His hede, his herte and his visage
Lich unto twenty winter age,
His hore haires were away,
And lich unto the fresshe May
Whan passed ben the colde shoures,
Right so recovereth he his floures.

Lo, what might any man devise,
A woman shewe in any wise
More hertely love in any stede
Than Medea to Jason dede?
First she made him the flees to winne,
And after that fro kith and kinne
With great tresor with him she stale,
And to his fader forth with all
His elde hath torned into youthe,
Which thing none other woman couthe.
But how it was to her aquit,
The remembraunce dwelleth yit.

King Peleus his eme was dede,
Jason bare croune upon his hede,
Medea hath fulfilled his will:
But whan he shuld of right fulfill
The trothe which to her afore
He had in thile of Colchos swore,
Tho was Medea most deceived.
For he an other hath received
Which doughter was to king Creon,
Creusa she hight, and thus Jason,

As he that was to love untrewe,
Medea left and toke a newe.
But that was after sone abought.
Medea with her art hath wrought
Of cloth of golde a mantel riche,
Which semeth worth a kinges riche,
And that was unto Creusa sent
In name of yeft and of present,
For susterhode hem was betwene.
And whan that yonge fresshe quene
That mantel lapped her aboute,
Anon therof the fire sprang oute
And brent her bothe flesshe and bon.
Tho cam Medea to Jason
With both his sones on her honde,
And said, 'O thou of every londe
The most untrewe creature,
Lo, this shall be thy forfeiture.'
With that she both his sones slough
Before his eye, and he out drough
His swerd and wold have slain her tho,
But farewell, she was ago
Unto Pallas the court above,
Where as she pleigneth upon love,
As she that was with that goddesse,
And he was lefte in great distresse.

PART TWO

[The Lover, in making his confession, tells the Confessor a great deal about his Lady and his love for her.]

I. HOURS IN THE BOWER

[BOOK IV, lines 1083–1244]

Among these other of Slouthes kinde,
Whiche alle labour set behinde,
And hateth alle besinesse,
There is yet one, whiche Idelnesse
Is cleped, and is the norice
In mannes kinde of every vice,
Which secheth eses many folde.
In winter doth he nought for colde,
In somer may he nought for hete;
So wether that he frese or swete,
Or be he in, or be he oute,
He woll ben idel al aboute,
But if he pleie ought at dees.
For who as ever take fees
And thenketh worship to deserve,
There is no lord whome he woll serve
As for to dwelle in his service,
But if it were in suche a wise,
Of that he seeth par aventure,
That by lordship and coverture
He may the more stonde stille,

And use his Idelnesse at wille.
For he ne woll no travail take
To ride for his ladi sake,
But liveth all upon his wisshes;
And as a cat wold ete fisshes
Withoute weting of his cles,
So wolde he do, but netheles
He faileth ofte of that he wolde.

'My sone, if thou of suche a molde
Art made, now tell me plein thy shrift.'

'Nay fader, god I yive a yift,
That toward Love, as by my wit
All idel was I never yit,
Ne never shall, while I may go.'

'Now, sone, telle me than so,
What hast thou done of besiship
To Love and to the ladyship
Of here which thy lady is?'

'My fader, ever yet er this
In every place, in every stede,
What so my lady hath me bede,
With all min herte obedient
I have therto be diligent.
And if so is that she bid nought,
What thing that than into my thought
Comth first, of that I may suffise,
I bowe and profre my service,
Sometime in chambre, sometime in halle,
Right so as I se the times falle.
And whan she goth to here masse
That time shall nought overpasse,

That I napproche her ladyhede
In aunter if I may her lede
Unto the chapel and ayein,
Than is nought all my wey in vein.
Somdele I may the better fare,
Whan I, that may nought fele her bare,
May lede her clothed in min arme.
But afterwarde it doth me harme
Of pure ymagination,
For thanne this collation
I make unto my selven ofte
And say: "Ha lord, how she is softe,
How she is round, how she is small,
Now wolde God, I hadde her all
Withoute daunger at my wille!"
And than I sike and sitte stille,
Of that I se my besy thought
Is torned idel into nought.
But for all that let I ne may,
Whan I se time another day,
That I ne do my besinesse
Unto my ladi worthinesse.
For I therto my wit affaite
To se the times and awaite
What is to done, and what to leve.
And so whan time is, by her leve,
What thing she bit me don, I do,
And where she bit me gon, I go,
And whan her list to clepe, I come.
Thus hath she fulliche overcome
Min idelnesse til I sterve,

So that I mot her nedes serve.
For as men sain, nede hath no lawe,
Thus mote I nedely to her drawe;
I serve, I bowe, I loke, I loute,
Min eye folweth her aboute.
What so she wolle so woll I,
Whan she woll sit, I knele by,
And whan she stont, than woll I stonde,
And whan she taketh her werk on honde
Of weving or of embrouderie,
Than can I nought but muse and prie
Upon her fingers longe and smale.
And nowe I thenke, and nowe I tale,
And nowe I singe, and nowe I sike,
And thus my contenaunce I pike.
And if it falle, as for a time
Her liketh nought abide by me
But busien her on other thinges,
Than make I other tarienges
To drecche forth the longe day,
For me is loth departe away.
And than I am so simple of port,
That for to feigne some desporte
I pleie with her litel hound
Nowe on the bed, nowe on the ground,
Now with the briddes in the cage,
For there is none so litel page
Ne yet so simple a chamberere,
That I ne make hem alle chere,
All for they shulde speke wele.
Thus mow ye se my besy whele,

That goth nought ideliche aboute.
And if her list to riden oute
On pelrinage or other stede,
I come, though I be nought bede,
And take her in min arme alofte
And set her in her sadel softe
And so forth lede her by the bridel,
For that I wolde nought ben idel.
And if her list to ride in chare,
And than I may therof beware,
Anone I shape me to ride
Right even by the chares side.
And as I may, I speke amonge,
And other while I singe a songe,
Whiche Ovide in his bokes made,
And said: "O whiche sorwes glad,
O which wofull prosperite
Belongeth to the proprete
Of Love, who so wold him serve!
And yet there fro may no man swerve,
That he ne mot his lawe obey."
And thus I ride forth my wey
And am right besy overall
With herte, and with my body all,
As I have saide you here to-fore.
My gode fader, tell therfore
Of Idelnesse if I have gilt.'
  'My sone, but thou telle wilt
Ought elles than I may now here,
Thou shalt have no penaunce here
And natheles a man may se,

How now a daies that there be
Full many of such hertes slowe,
That woll nought besien hem to knowe
What thing Love is, til ate last,
That he with strengthe hem overcast
That malgre hem thei mot obey
And done all idelship awey
To serve wel and besiliche.
But, sone, thou art none of sich,
For Love shall thee wel excuse.
But otherwise if thou refuse
To love, thou might so par cas
Ben idel, as somtime was
A kinges doughter unavised,
Til that Cupide her hath chastised,
Wherof thou shalt a tale here
Accordant unto this matere.'

[*Here follows the* Tale of Rosiphelee.]

II. THE LONG NIGHTS

[BOOK IV, lines 2771–2926]

'For certes, fader Genius,
Yet unto now it hath be thus,
At alle time if it befelle
So that I mighte come and dwelle
In place there my lady were,
I was nought slow ne slepy there.
For than I dare well undertake,
That whan her list on nightes wake
In chambre as to carole and daunce,

Me thenketh I may me more avaunce
If I may gone upon her honde,
Than if I wonne a kinges londe.
For whan I may her hond beclippe,
With such gladnesse I daunce and skippe
Me thenketh I touche nought the floor;
The roo, which renneth on the moor,
Is thanne nought so light as I.
So mow ye witen all forthy,
That for the time slepe I hate.
And whan it falleth other gate,
So that her like nought to daunce,
But on the dees to caste chaunce,
Or axe of Love some demaunde,
Or elles that her list commaunde
To rede and here of Troilus,
Right as she wold, or so or thus,
I am all redy to consent.
And if so is, that I may hent
Somtime amonge a good leisir,
So as I dare of my desir
I telle a part; but whan I prey,
Anone she biddeth me go my wey
And saith: "It is fer in the night:"
And I swere, it is even light.
But as it falleth ate laste,
There may no worldes joie laste,
So mote I nedes fro her wende
And of my wacche make an ende.
And if she thanne hede toke
How pitouslich on her I loke,

Whan that I shall my leve take,
Her ought of mercy for to slake
Her daunger, which saith ever nay.
But he saith often, "Have good day,"
That loth is for to take his leve.
Therfore while I may beleve,
I tarie forth the night alonge.
For it is nought on me alonge
To slepe that I so soone go
Till that I mote algate so;
And thanne I bidde: "God her se,"
And so down knelende on my kne
I take leve, and if I shall,
I kisse her, and go forth withall.
And other while, if that I dore,
Er I come fully ate dore,
I torne ayein and feigne a thing,
As though I hadde lost a ring
Or somwhat elles, for I wolde
Kisse her eftsone, if that I sholde.
But selden is that I so spede.
And whan I se that I mot nede
Departen, I departe, and thanne
With all my herte I curse and banne
That ever slepe was made for eye.
For as me thenketh I might drie
Withoute slepe to waken ever,
So that I shulde nought dissever
Fro her, in whom is all my light.
And than I curse also the night
With all the will of my corage

And say: "Away thou black ymage,
Which of thy derke cloudy face
Makest all the worldes light deface
And causest unto slepe a way,
By which I mot now gone away
Out of my ladi compaignie.
O slepy night, I thee defie,
And wolde that thou lay in presse
With Proserpine the goddesse
And with Pluto the helle king.
For till I se the daies spring,
I sette slepe nought at a risshe."
And with that worde I sigh and wisshe
And say: "Ha, why ne were it day?
For yet my lady than I may
Beholde, though I do no more."

*   *   *   *   *

But slepe, I not wherof it serveth,
Of which no man his thank deserveth
To get him love in any place,
But is an hindrer of his grace
And maketh hem dede as for a throwe
Right as a stoke were overthrowe.
And so, my fader, in this wise
The slepy nightes I despise,
And ever amiddes of my tale
I thenke upon the nightingale,
Which slepeth nought by wey of kinde
For love, in bokes as I finde.
Thus ate last I go to bedde

And yet min herte lith to wedde
With her where as I came fro;
Though I departe he woll nought so,
There is no lock may shet him out,
Him nedeth nought to gon about
That perce may the harde wal;
Thus is he with her overall,
And thus my selven I torment,
Til that the dede slepe me hent.
But thanne by a thousand score
Wel more than I was to-fore
I am tormented in my slepe,
But that I dreme is nought on shepe,
For I ne thenke nought on wulle,
But I am drecched to the fulle
Of Love, that I have to kepe,
That now I laugh and now I wepe
And now I lese and now I winne
And now I ende and now beginne.
And other while I dreme and mete,
That I alone with her mete
And that Daunger is left behinde.
And than in slepe such joy I finde,
That I ne bede never awake.
But after, whan I hede take,
And shall arise upon the morwe,
Than is all torned into sorwe,
Nought for the cause I shall arise,
But for I mette in suche a wise,
And ate last I am bethought,
That all is vein and helpeth nought:

But yet me thenketh by my wille
I wold have lay and slepe stille
To meten ever of such a sweven,
For than I had a slepy heven.'
   'My sone, and for thou tellest so,
A man may finde of time ago,
That many a sweven hath be certain,
All be it so, that som men sain
That swevens ben of no credence.
But for to shewe in evidence
That they full ofte sothe thinges
Betoken, I thenke in my writinges
To telle a tale therupon,
Which fell by olde daies gone.'

   [*For the story which follows see the*
   Tale of Ceix and Alceone, *p.* 17.]

III. IN CHURCH

[BOOK V, lines 7030–7194]

   'Lo thus, where sacrilegge is used,
A man can feigne his conscience:
And right upon such evidence
In Loves cause if I shall trete,
There ben of suche small and great,
If they no leiser finden elles
They wol nought wonden for the belles,
Ne though they sen the prest at masse;
That wol they leten overpasse,
If that they finden her love there
They stande and tellen in her ere,

And axe of God none other grace
While they ben in that holy place.
But er they gon some avauntage
There will they have, and some pilage
Of goodly word or of beheste,
Or elles they take ate leste
Out of her honde a ring or glove,
So nigh the weder they will hove,
As who saith she shall nought foryete,
Now I this token of her have gete.
Thus halwe they the highe feste,
Such thefte may no chirch areste,
For all is lefull that hem liketh,
To whom that elles it misliketh.
And eke right in the selve kinde
In greate citees men may finde
This lusty folk, that make hem gay,
And waite upon the haliday,
In chirches and in minstres eke
They gon the women for to seke,
And where that such one goth about
To-fore the fairest of the route
Where as they sitten all a rewe,
There will he moste his body shewe,
His croket kempt and theron set
An ouche with a chapelet,
Or elles one of grene leves,
Which late came oute of the greves,
All for he shulde seme fressh.
And thus he loketh on his flessh,
Right as an hawke which hath a sight

Upon the fowl there he shall light;
And as he were a fairie,
He sheweth him to-fore her eye
In holy place where they sitte,
Al for to make her hertes flitte.
His eye no where woll abide
But loke and pry on every side
On her and her, as him best liketh:
And other while among he siketh;
Thenketh one of hem "That was for me!"
And so there thenken two or thre
And yet he loveth none of alle,
But where as ever his chaunce falle.
And netheles to say a soth
The cause why that he so doth,
Is for to stele an herte or two
Out of the chirche er that he go.
And as I said it here above,
All is that sacrilegge of love,
For well may be he steleth awey
That he never after yelde may.
Tell me forthy, my sone, anone,
Hast thou do sacrilegge or none
As I have said in this manere?'
   'My fader, as of this matere
I woll you tellen redely
What I have do; but truely
I may excuse min entent,
That I never yet to chirche went
In such maner as ye me shrive,
For no woman that is on live.

The cause why I have it laft
May be for I unto that craft
Am nothing able for to stele,
Though there be women nought so fele.
But yet woll I nought saie this,
Whan I am there my lady is,
In whom lith holy my quarele,
And she to chirche or to chapele
Woll go to matins or to messe,—
That time I waite well and gesse,
To chirche I come, and there I stonde,
And though I take a boke on honde
My contenaunce is on the boke,
But toward her is all my loke.
And if so falle, that I pray
Unto my God and somwhat say
Of *Pater Noster* or of Crede
All is for that I wolde spede,
So that my bede in holy chirche
There mighte some miracle wirche
My ladies herte for to chaunge,
Which ever hath be to me so straunge;
So that all my devocion
And all my contemplacion
With all min herte and my corage
Is only set on her ymage.
And ever I waite upon the tide
If she loke any thing aside,
That I me may of her avise;
Anone I am with covetise
So smite, that me were lefe

To be in holy chirche a thefe,
But nought to stele a vestement
For that is nothing my talent.
But I wol stele, if that I might,
A glad word or a goodly sight,
And ever my service I profre,
And namely whan she woll gone offre,
For than I lede her, if I may,
For somwhat wold I stele away.
Whan I beclippe her on the waste,
Yet ate last I stele a taste,
And other while "graunt mercy"
She saith, and so win I therby
A lusty touch, a good worde eke,
But all the remenaunt to seke
Is fro my purpos wonder fer.
So may I say, as I said er,
In holy chirch if that I wowe,
My conscience I wolde allowe
Be so that up amendement
I mighte get assignement
Where for to spede in other place;
Such sacrilegge I hold a grace.
  'And thus, my fader, soth to say,
In chirche right as in the way
If I might ought of love take
Such hansel have I nought forsake.
But finally I me confesse,
There is in me no halinesse
While I her se in haly stede.
And yet, for ought that ever I dede,

No sacrilegge of her I toke
But if it were of worde or loke,
Or elles if that I her fredde
Whan I toward offring her ledde,
Take therof what I take may
For elles bere I nought away:
For though I wolde ought elles have,
All other thinges ben so save
And kept with such a privilegge
That I may do no sacrilegge;
God wot my wille natheles.
Though I must nedes kepe pees
And malgre min so let it passe,
My will therto is nought the lasse,
If I might other wise away.
Forthy, my fader, I you pray,
Tell what you thenketh therupon,
If I therof have gilt or none.'
　'Thy will, my sone, is for to blame,
The remenaunt is but a game
That I have herd the telle yit.
But take this lore into thy wit,
That alle thing hath time and stede,
The chirche serveth for the bede,
The chambre is of an other speche;
But if thou wistest of the wreche
How sacrilegge it hath abought,
Thou woldest better ben bethought.
And for thou shalt the more amende,
A tale I will on the despende.'

[*Here follows the* Tale of Paris and Helen.]

CAMBRIDGE
Printed by W. LEWIS, M.A.
at the University Press